FROM ASHES ON TO LIFE

Lenten Sermons
And Hymns

BY CHARLES J. CURLEY

C.S.S Publishing Co., Inc.
Lima, Ohio

FROM ASHES ON TO LIFE

Library of Congress Cataloging-in-Publication Data

Curley, Charles J., 1945-
    From ashes on to life : Lenten sermons and hymns / by Charles J. Curley.
        p.   cm.
    ISBN 1-55673-386-0
    I. Lenten sermons.   2. Presbyterian Church—Sermons. 3. Sermons, American. 4. Lenten hymns.   5. Lent—Prayer-books and devotions—English.   I.   Title.
BV4277.C85   1992
252'.62—dc20   91-28453
                                                                              CIP

9204 / ISBN 1-55673-386-0   PRINTED IN U.S.A.

To

Jill

for her

patience
encouragement
love

TABLE OF CONTENTS

INTRODUCTION

This book of sermons and services for Lent was written from the conviction that worship begins with, ends with and is centered in the Word of God read, interpreted, prayed and sung in the congregation. It is a sad thing when worship degenerates into a stringing together of isolated elements: music, prayers, sermon, with no unifying theme growing out of the Scripture. The Scripture text, and only the Scripture text, gives life and wholeness to our worship. It has been my experience that this integration of the elements of the worship service around the Scripture most often breaks down when it comes time to select the music. Even with the proliferation of modern hymnody, when available for congregational singing, there is a "neutral" flavor to many of the hymns we sing.

Is it worthwhile to write hymns so specific to a particular text that they are essentially written for "one-time use?" I think so. It is my hope that this small book will encourage preachers to consider becoming writers of hymns as well as sermons. When we are at our best we "preach" through the entire service. Many times I have stepped out of the pulpit acknowledging that the words sung have penetrated the consciousness of the congregation in a way that my spoken words have not.

Finally, this is a book for a particular season. A biblical call to worship, prayer of confession, Scripture text, hymn and sermon is offered for each Sunday, with more extensive services, and a number of hymns, for Maundy Thursday and Good Friday. I am especially grateful for the patience and the encouragement of the people of West Presbyterian Church in Binghamton, New York, and University Presbyterian Church in Rochester Hills, Michigan, where these services and sermons, and more recently the hymns, had their birth in the worship life of these two faithful congregations.

ASH WEDNESDAY

Call To Worship
Prayer Of Confession
Hymn
Sermon

ASH WEDNESDAY

Call To Worship
Adapted From Psalm 51

L: Create in me a clean heart, O God,

R: Put a new and right spirit within me.

L: Cast me not away from your presence,

R: And take not your Holy Spirit from me.

L: Deliver me from guilt, O God, you God of my salvation.

R: O Lord, open my lips, and my mouth shall show forth your praise,

L: For I have no delight in sacrifice; were I to give a burnt offering, you would not be pleased.

R: The sacrifice acceptable to God is a broken spirit; a broken and contrite heart, O God, you will not despise.

ASH WEDNESDAY

Prayer Of Confession

Almighty God, forgive us when we yield to despair, and give way to darkness. Forgive us when we act as if our salvation depended on ourselves alone. Forgive us when we do not trust you enough to see hope even in loss, light at the end of our darkness. O Lord, in your refining fire burn away our doubt and hesitation, turn despair to ashes and lead us on to life. Amen.

Scripture: Isaiah 63:17—64:8

ASH WEDNESDAY

Hymn
[Tune: St. Christopher, often sung as
"Beneath the Cross of Jesus"]

1. Forgive, O Lord, your people, forgive us all our sins,
   May they be burned to ashes, like dust upon the wind.
   And vanish in the bright new dawn of your eternal love,
   That banishes our darkness and lifts our hearts above.

2. Our Lenten journey calls us, to follow on Christ's way;
   Repented, changed, forgiven, we look to God's new day.
   Our old ways left behind us now, so full of storm and strife,
   We follow Christ our savior, from ashes on to life. Amen.

ASH WEDNESDAY

Sermon

"Yet . . ."

"Yet, O Lord, thou art our Father;
we are the clay, and thou art our potter;"
Isaiah 64:8

These words of the prophet Isaiah speak of agony and hopelessness bracketed by faith. The most important word of this text is "yet" (64:8) . . . "yet, thou art our Father" — repeating at the end of the Scripture lesson the same affirmation made at the beginning, an affirmation of faith made in spite of the fact that there is absolutely no external evidence of any sort to support it. An affirmation of faith made in spite of the fact that there is not one single thing left in the life of this captive people to suggest to them that they could possibly be cared for by a loving God, who loved them like a father. In fact, once that affirmation is made at the beginning, the whole movement of the text is downward into despair.

For this people, all the supports of community, continuity, promise and tradition have been taken away. More than that, the exile itself seemed to demonstrate that either God no longer loved them, or that God no longer had power to protect them. Either way, for them everything was gone — hopes and dreams were gone, faith was gone. I can't think of any analogy in our communal life today which would help us understand the enormity of the loss they experienced. Not only did it seem God had left them, it called into question whether God had been with them in the first place:

> "We have become like those over whom thou
> hast never ruled, like those who are not
> called by thy name (63:19)."

14

This is more than a passing depression or a dark night of the soul. There is nothing left!

> "We have all become unclean . . .
> all our righteous deeds are polluted . . .
> we all fade like a leaf, and our iniquities,
>   like the wind, take us away (64:6)."

There is nothing left! Nothing but that one little "yet" in verse eight.

That "yet," "yet, O Lord, thou art our father," brings us full circle back to faith. We are indeed "nothing," but we are "nothing" in the hands of the creator who fashioned an entire universe out of "nothing." "Yet, thou O Lord art our father; we are the clay and thou art our potter." In his hands we are never lost. It is the skill of the potter alone which can see in a glop of mud the lovely creation which will emerge when that mud is worked upon the wheel. It is the love of God that can take the deepest darkness and despair life can throw at us, and then remold our lives into new creations.

The message of Lent is also one of agony and hopelessness bracketed by faith, for the great triumph of the resurrection emerges out of the "nothingness" of the cross. On Good Friday, all hopes were shattered, all faith turned to ashes. On the cross, everything was stripped away from Jesus and he was left with the despair of: "My God, my God, why hast thou forsaken me?" Yet . . . yet in that cross was our salvation. God worked in the darkness and with the despair to redeem mankind. God's love brought us from ashes to life. In the "yet . . ." is our salvation.

FIRST SUNDAY IN LENT

Call To Worship
Prayer Of Confession
Hymn
Sermon

FIRST SUNDAY IN LENT

Call To Worship
From Deuteronomy 8:1-3

L: All that I command you this day you shall do,

R: **That you may live and multiply and possess the land which the Lord swore to give to you.**

L: And you shall remember all the way which the Lord your God has led you these 40 years in the wilderness,

R: **That he might humble you, testing you to know what was in your heart.**

L: And he humbled you and let you hunger and fed you with manna,

R: **That he might make you know that man does not live by bread alone, but by everything that proceeds out of the mouth of the Lord.**

FIRST SUNDAY IN LENT

Prayer Of Confession

Help us, Lord, when we are tempted to do only what is expected of us. Forgive us when we pursue the illusions of power and the deceptions of security. We have wasted our lives on bread that does not satisfy. Heal us, renew us, and feed us with Living Bread, that we might do the unexpected deed of love and speak the elusive word of peace. Amen.

Scripture: Luke 4:1-13

FIRST SUNDAY IN LENT

Hymn
[Tune: Old 124th, often sung as
"Turn Back O Man"]

1. In deepest wilderness for 40 days,
   Led by the Spirit, Jesus fasts and prays;
   Led to the Tempter in the final hour,
   Tested and tried by visions of great power,
   Jesus is tempted in so many ways.

2. Tempted to feed a hungry world with bread,
   Tempted to rule just as the Scriptures said,
   On angel wings borne up without a care,
   Jesus, my Lord, the Tempter's words beware.
   Sell not your soul for power, life or bread.

3. Temptation's hour is not to be denied.
   Temptation's power is magnified by pride.
   Tempted to be what all expect of me,
   To be the best of all that I can see.
   Temptation's power is not to be denied.

4. Temptation's power is broken by the Lord.
   Temptation's hour can never be ignored.
   To give up all that I could ever be,
   Into the hands of one greater than me.
   Temptation's power is broken by my Lord. Amen.

FIRST SUNDAY IN LENT

Sermon

"The Devil Quotes Scripture Too"

"And Jesus . . . was led by the spirit for
40 days in the wilderness
tempted by the devil."
Luke 4:1-2

I will always remember the immortal words of Flip Wilson's "Geraldine:" "The devil made me do it!" She said those words with a gleam in her eye which let you know just how enjoyable yielding to temptation really was. Temptation has come on hard times in our day. It has come to mean little more than resistance to a hot-fudge sundae when you are on a diet, or turning down a piece of chocolate cake. At most, resisting temptation seems to mean no more than the self-discipline it takes to stay away from something we know is bad for us.

Each year the lectionary begins Lent with the story of Jesus' temptation, after 40 days in the wilderness. Perhaps this is done in order to remind us that it might possibly be a healthy thing for us to walk through the wilderness and learn to face temptation as well. This may seem a strange suggestion, since common sense would say that the best way to avoid yielding to temptation would be to stay away from it whenever possible. But who, after all, sent Jesus to be tempted? The gospels say, variously, that Jesus was led, driven or dragged into the wilderness by the Spirit of God. Jesus was led to temptation by the same God who, only a short time before, at his baptism, had declared: "This is my beloved Son!"

22

In that deathly and dangerous wilderness, what terrible things was Jesus tempted to do? Let's take a moment to set a ground rule here: to be a temptation, something must be tempting. This may not be as obvious as it seems. For example, my children, who freely offer to give up the temptation of spinach for Lent. If it is not tempting, if it does not have some real and strong attraction for you in the first place, it cannot be called a temptation! With what did the devil tempt Jesus? "If you are the Son of God, command this stone to become bread." Bread? He was hungry and his world was hungry, here was his chance: "Jesus, I know you're the Son of God, and you know you're the Son of God, but since we're out here all by ourselves in this wilderness and you need a bite to eat and there are no grocery stores handy — why don't you just turn these stones to bread — nobody else will see but us."

Interestingly enough, Jesus answers by quoting Moses in Deuteronomy 8, when he was remembering how the people of Israel failed to trust God to feed them in the wilderness, and God had to give them manna to keep them from fleeing back to Egypt. So Jesus says: "Man shall not live by bread alone." But if not, then by what? Well, for one thing, in the wilderness by the promise that God would bring them through safely. The temptation is for us not to trust in God, but to make sure. I see this temptation in the prosperity preachers of television evangelism, who say that if you only believe in God enough, everything in your life will be wonderful; and, if everything is not wonderful, that means you do not believe in God enough. This is the same temptation Jesus rejected: the temptation not to trust God when times are tough. Especially in the wilderness do we need to trust God day-by-day to bring us through.

When Jesus does not buy the devil's pitch for prosperity ("all the bread you can eat"), next the devil tries to tempt him with power — power to do good. "You can have all the power you want, think of all the good you will be able to do with so much power." Even the church has felt this temptation, and has often yielded to it. But it is so tempting to think you might be able to shape the destiny of the world, change the course of history. It was tempting to medieval popes and their armies, to 19th century missionaries, to social justice advocates of the left and the moral majority of the right. And all would use that power for good, of course. But Jesus says no, no to power.

Finally, the devil quotes Scripture at Jesus one last time — which proves the truth of the old saying I have used as the title of this sermon. And it is interesting, though I don't know exactly what it means, that while Jesus quotes Deuteronomy loosely, the devil quotes Psalm 91 quite accurately. What is the temptation here? What possible appeal could there be for Jesus to throw himself off the pinnacle of the temple? To know that he is invincible, that nothing could ever hurt him? If you knew that, what would you ever have to fear? It certainly would give you a tremendous sense of security.

The devil, in fact, tempts Jesus with good things, not bad. The devil tempts Jesus with things we would all like. All three temptations fit popular expectations of the Messiah; that the Messiah would be a Moses who would feed the people, a David ruling in peace and justice and a Son of Man carried along on clouds of glory. This was what everyone knew the Messiah would be. Everyone except Jesus.

I believe that in the temptation the devil performed a very important function for God. The devil tempted Jesus to be what all the people (from their study of Scripture) expected he would be. The devil offers these temptations to Jesus one by one, giving him the opportunity to reject them before they are offered to him, much more subtly and ever so much more dangerously, in the adoring voices of his followers. We all know how easy it is to be trapped by others' expectations of us. People around us expect us to act in a certain way, and by and large we do; even, at times, against our better judgment. Jesus was vulnerable also. The devil did God's will by bringing before Jesus the temptations he needed to confront. The real danger was not that he would yield to these temptations in the wilderness, but that by failing to confront them

24

there he would, without being aware it was happening, find himself acquiescing to these same temptations out in the world, during his ministry — thereby slipping bit by bit into the devil's control.

I doubt that anyone, before they take their first drink, makes the decision: "I'm going to be an alcoholic." It is just that one drink follows another because "everybody's doing it" until they are trapped. Who would choose to be addicted to drugs? They just pop a few pills or sniff a little cocaine because it feels good and it's the thing to do, and their dependence elevates step by step until they are trapped. This is a different way of understanding temptation. It is not the same as simply having the moral fortitude to avoid something you know is bad for you. The devil tempts with the most exalted hopes in the world. The devil tempts Jesus with what everyone around him knows is the will of God for Jesus. But in this case it is yesterday's will of God, and God is leading Jesus in a different direction entirely.

The way of prosperity, power and protection is not for him. His is the way of service, suffering and sacrifice. Everybody knows that God wants him to succeed — but Jesus knows that God wants him to be the servant of all. Everybody knows that there is a throne in Jesus' future, and a golden crown — Jesus knows that his throne is the cross and his only crown of thorns. Everybody knows that Jesus is meant to rule the earth (and they are to rule with him) — Jesus knows that he is to give his life for the salvation of the world and that they, too, must die to their old lives to live for God.

It is so easy to be tempted by what "everybody knows;" to be caught by what everybody expects we will be and do in this life. It is a temptation we just find ourselves sliding into bit by bit, until one day we wake up to find we're feeling sort of cynical and jaded about life and that we have forgotten the promises of God who called us out of the wilderness and promised to make us a new creation altogether. This is the worst temptation of all — to be tempted away from hope. In Jesus Christ, God came into the world to do a new thing —

an unexpected thing. In Jesus Christ, God came into the world to call people like you and like me, even when we are in the wilderness, to live a life of service, of grateful acceptance of God's love. Jesus calls us to a life full of hope for the future and the expectation that God will do, even in us, a new thing. It is the temptation to forget all this as we find our own way through life that makes the devil so dangerous.

SECOND SUNDAY IN LENT

Call To Worship
Prayer Of Confession
Hymn
Sermon

SECOND SUNDAY IN LENT

Call To Worship
From John 1:14-17

L: And the Word became flesh and dwelt among us, full of grace and truth;

R: **We have beheld his glory, glory as of the only Son from the Father.**

L: And from his fullness have we all received, grace upon grace.

R: **For the law was given through Moses, grace and truth came through Jesus Christ.**

SECOND SUNDAY IN LENT

Prayer Of Confession

Lord our God, you know how much we love the glory of the mountaintop, but fear the valley with the shadow of the cross. Forgive us, and help us serve your people in the midst of the pain and anxiety of this world with all the life that we have been given. Transfigure us, we pray, that our world may become a new creation in Jesus Christ our Lord. Amen.

Scripture: Luke 9:28-36

SECOND SUNDAY IN LENT

Hymn
[Tune: Lancashire, often sung as
"Lead On O King Eternal"]

1. They followed to the mountain, they followed Christ their
     Lord,
   And there beheld God's glory, as light around him poured.
   In company with prophets, with heroes of the Word,
   In this transfiguration, God's voice on earth is heard.

2. Disciples came to Jesus to beg that they might stay,
   And there upon the mountain, relive the glorious day.
   But not in mountain's grandeur, nor glory like the sun,
   Will God be found incarnate, while his work is undone.

3. We follow to the valley, we follow full of fears;
   A cross waits in the future, a time of pain and tears.
   Yet living out the vision, his story we will tell;
   God's glory never fails us, transfigures us as well. Amen.

SECOND SUNDAY IN LENT

Sermon

"To The Mountain"

". . . he took with him Peter
and John and James, and went up
on to the mountain to pray."
Luke 9:28

The story of the transfiguration of Jesus often seems like a way-station in Lent — a surprising oasis that catches us off guard after the sun-parched desolation of the temptation in the wilderness. Yet this story of God's glory poured out on Jesus on the mountain is only a brief respite on the weary way to the cross. We never seem to fully grasp what it is all about, and it is soon forgotten as we journey on through the more familiar pathways of Lent. We, after all, know that Lent is not about glory, Lent is not about life — don't we? But why is that? Why do we assume that Lent is only about death — and we have to wait for Easter to talk about life? Why do we assume that suffering must come first, so that reward can follow? Why do we insist that there must be no break in the bleak inevitability impelling Jesus to Jerusalem and the cross? In spite of all we believe, here stands the transfiguration in the midst of Lent, like a feast in the middle of a long dry fast.

What happened that day on the mountain, in this story of light and spirit and heroes long since dead? Who knows? I certainly can't say I understand the transfiguration, even though I have read many scholarly accounts which try to rationalize the transfiguration into something understandable: . . . it was a dream, . . . a story made up by the disciples after the resurrection, . . . a vision, a hallucination, . . . and on and on. Not one of these feeble attempts comes close to touching the power of that event. Does it matter that we do not understand? Not even Peter, who was there, understood! The issue is not understanding, or even believing, the issue is transfiguration — of Jesus, of the disciples, and our transfiguration as well! And transfiguration, for us, is something we seldom experience in our lives. And those few times when some mighty change comes upon us, transfigures us, are often not the most welcome times in our lives.

It sometimes seems to me that there is far too much emphasis on belief in the Christian religion — on intellectual assent or emotional commitment. And far too little attention paid to action. Moses went up a mountain and there the glory of the Lord was revealed to him. The purpose of that revelation was not to change Moses, to make him more spiritual, more loving, more sensitive. The purpose of that revelation was to transfigure the way of living of the whole people of God. So it is with Jesus.

It is no more an accident that we read this story in the midst of Lent than it was that the story was recorded in the gospels in the midst of experiences of suffering and prophecies of death. And that is just where the revelation of God's glory belongs. Jesus did not take a mountaintop vacation to "get away from it all" — to escape, to rest, to be renewed. Jesus was transfigured on the mountain to meet the challenge waiting for him back down in the valley. The transfiguration was not meant to be looked back on nostalgically as a "break" from the suffering of the world, but to be seen as a gift in God's grace impelling Jesus deeper and deeper into the pain and darkness of a suffering world — until that pain and darkness culminated in the cross.

Peter, James and John could not understand on the mountain that God's glory was not to be found apart from the suffering world in the valley. Peter wanted to build "booths" to stay on the mountain, to bask in the glory. But the blinding light on the mountaintop was a declaration of the presence of the glory of God in the world. That glory is not something you wait for, hope for, seek for — that glory of God is already present in the midst of a tired, aching world, wherever God's people do God's work. The transfiguration is not a vision of the way the world could be, it is a declaration of the way the world already is, when God's people accept the promise and live out the vision.

Peter wanted to stay on the mountaintop and bask in God's glory. Jesus knew that God's glory was not on the mountain, but down in the valley where an epileptic boy waited to be healed, the disciples were arguing about who would be greatest in the kingdom, and Lazarus, Jesus' friend, was dying. God's glory was down in the valley where a cross waited on a Friday called Good. This is the glory of God, transfiguring the world.

Some years ago, I took part in the funeral of a minister, who was one year younger than I. In the midst of tears, there was life. He had died in faith, surrounded by a loving congregation brought together by his dying. In the love which that congregation shared with him and his family, far beyond any requirement or expectation, for his last year, there was life. In some way, all of us who lived through his last, hard year, were transfigured. The glory of God is all around us, even on the way to the cross. Peter wanted to stay on the mountain and live in the moment of glory forever, but it could not be. Life moves on, and the way of Jesus moved on to the cross. Moments of transformation are not to be held on to, but are to change you to live on in a different way, even after the light is gone. The question in every transfiguration, every conversion, every burst of enthusiasm, is: does it change us and enable us to live better the lives to which we are called? Believing is only the beginning.

The transfiguration of Jesus is not an oasis, a temporary resting place in the gospels, but a sign of the presence of God's glory, alive in our world — and it is not by our words, nor by our beliefs that the reality of that glory will be judged in our lives, but by the transfiguration caused in us, our lives and our actions, when we behold the glory of God.

THIRD SUNDAY IN LENT

Call To Worship
Prayer Of Confession
Hymn
Sermon

THIRD SUNDAY IN LENT

Call To Worship
Adapted From Psalm 130

L: Out of the depths I cry to you, O Lord.

R: Lord, hear my voice!

L: Let your ears be attentive to the voice of my supplications!

R: If you, O Lord, should mark iniquities, who could stand?

L: But there is forgiveness with the Lord.

R: I wait for the Lord, my soul waits, and in his word I hope;

L: My soul waits for the Lord more than watchmen for the morning.

R: More than watchmen for the morning do I wait for the Lord.

THIRD SUNDAY IN LENT

Prayer Of Confession

As we journey through Lent, Lord, we confess that we have often been less than willing pilgrims on your way. Sometimes, we have waited too long, paralyzed when you have called us to action. Other times we have acted precipitously, busying ourselves to hide the emptiness within. Attune us to your call, Lord of life. Help us to do what is right, to hear your voice, and to walk in your ways. Amen.

Scripture: John 5:1-9

THIRD SUNDAY IN LENT

Hymn
[Tune: Hamburg, often sung as
"When I Survey the Wondrous Cross"]

1. Lord, come and hear your people's prayers,
   Our voices raised to praise your name.
   In your great love we rest our cares,
   And find forgiveness for our shame.

2. More than the watchman upon the wall,
   More than the sinner by Bethesda's pool,
   Waiting, we yearn to hear your call,
   'til we surrender to your rule.

3. Stir up the waters of our lives,
   'til we walk finally in your ways;
   Healed, loved, renewed, made strong and wise,
   To be disciples all our days. Amen.

THIRD SUNDAY IN LENT

Sermon

"Waiting By The Healing Waters"

"Do you want to be healed?"
John 5:6

"Do you want to be healed?" That is all Jesus asked him, as he lay there on his pallet, among the others, all the others waiting to be healed: "a multitude of invalids, blind, lame, paralyzed, waiting for the moving of the water (5:3)." He lay there day after day, waiting for someone to help him into the waters, for he didn't need to get to the waters any old time, but in that particular time when the waters were moving. Bethesda was a pool fed by deep springs which occasionally moved the waters. Legend had it that at those times an angel was stirring up the waters, and if you could get in while the waters were moving, then you would be healed. Did it work? Who are we to say? Though I am obviously skeptical — he never got there fast enough to find out. But at least waiting by the waters gave him hope. At least it was doing something, and doing something is always better than doing nothing, isn't it?

Doing nothing is frustrating. Times when we are forced to do nothing are particularly infuriating. Think of the families of those held hostage in Lebanon. Think of the frustration of their long wait — some for years! Then another hostage is taken, and another, and we demand that the government do something! So the government lodges a protest and rattles swords and moves battleships — and nothing much is accomplished, but it's doing something, and doing something is always better than doing nothing, isn't it?

40

From time to time in my life I have been involved with groups having pretty grand objectives; big goals like: "No more war, ever again!" or "Feed all the world's hungry. Eliminate poverty in our lifetime." Yet time and again good intentions have been frustrated by the enormity of the problem, and our objectives have shrunk, getting smaller and smaller, until: "Well, we didn't stamp out poverty, in fact, there are more poor people now than when we started, but at least we made folks aware that there's a problem." And we have been content, for at least we did something, and doing something is always better than doing nothing, isn't it?

From time to time various denominations develop a new evangelism program. We receive letters about it with a whole stack of multi-colored brochures and a couple of posters. The letters say something like this: "If churches will give their full support to this program it will lead to the dawning of a new day for our denomination, of new life for our church." And then I think of all the other programs in the 1980s and the 1970s and the 1960s, all promising that this program or that program would change the church and the world in a year or a decade . . . but at least it's doing something, and doing something is always better than doing nothing, isn't it?

As I look back at my life, and at the life of our nation and our church, I find that the need to do something comes at those times when we are most paralyzed; at the times when the American militlary/political/industrial giant really is helpless to stop terrorists, end the flow of drugs, eliminate hunger — "but we've got to do something!" We've lived through the New Frontier, the Great Society, and every other federal poverty program to come down the pike; and the poor keep getting poorer, and we've run out of ideas. We watch our cities deteriorate, become battlegrounds, and we're helpless, paralyzed.

The Bible recognizes many kinds of paralysis. When Jesus heals a blind man, John reminds us that there is no one as blind as the person who fails to see that this is God's son. The Bible often reminds us that spiritual paralysis, which allows us to see the will of God but not do it, is worse than any physical affliction. The Bible sees very little difference between a withered arm and a withered spirit. To understand this story from John's gospel, of the pool of Bethesda, we must understand that we, too, are lying by the waters, waiting for the moving of the waters, waiting for someone to carry us to the waters. How often have you found yourself by the pool — paralyzed — unable to move.

I had a depressing experience some time ago. I was asked to visit a church in another community where there were "problems." A small group of the congregation was very unhappy with their minister. I met with that group and the church board. What I found depressing was that during the meeting everyone who spoke had a complaint: this was wrong and that was wrong. No one spoke up to say, "If we just pull together, we can solve our problems." Yet after the meeting, five different people came to me privately to say: "They're wrong, things aren't so bad — we can work it out." So I asked them, "Why didn't you speak up?" They replied, "I don't like to argue." "I'm kind of shy in groups." "I'm not sure of myself enough to stand up and say something." Paralysis! We hesitate to speak, we wait to see if problems will go away on their own, we wait until we don't feel timid, we wait like withered people beside the pool, thinking that anyway, we're still here, and that's doing something! And doing something is always better than doing nothing! What did Jesus do? Jesus did not do something! Had Jesus done "something" he would have done what the paralyzed man wanted . . . do you remember what he wanted? Had Jesus done "something," he would have helped the paralyzed man into the pool when the waters were moving — for that, after all, is what he wanted. It might not have done any good, but at least it would have been doing something. But that is just what Jesus did not do! Jesus did not do something, Jesus did the thing, the one thing, the exact thing that needed doing! "Do you want to be healed? Rise, take up your pallet and walk (5:8)."

FOURTH
SUNDAY
IN LENT

Call To Worship
Prayer Of Confession
Hymn
Sermon

FOURTH SUNDAY IN LENT

Call To Worship
Adapted From Mark and Matthew passages

L: Jesus said: "What do you want me to do for you?" A Leper replied:

R: **"If you will, you can make me clean."**

L: A Centurion asked:

R: **"Only say the word, and my servant will be healed."**

L: A Woman declared:

R: **"If I touch even his garments, I shall be made well."**

L: Jarius begged:

R: **"My daughter has just died, come and lay your hand on her and she will live."**

L: And Bartimaeus, the blind beggar of Jericho, said to Jesus:

R: **"Master, let me receive my sight."**

FOURTH SUNDAY IN LENT

Prayer Of Confession

Lord Jesus. Son of God. Have mercy on us. As we pass through our lives, hear us. Forgive us for the ways in which we have been blind to the needs of others: spouse and family, neighbors and friends, the poor and the oppressed. Forgive us for our blindness which takes no responsibility for the consequences of our own actions or for the sickness of our society. We have closed our eyes and hardened our hearts. We are blind to everything we would rather not see. Jesus. Son of God. Have mercy on us. Amen.

Assurance Of Forgiveness (Mark 10:52): "Go your way; your faith has made you well."

Scripture: Mark 10:46-52

FOURTH SUNDAY IN LENT

Hymn — Bartimaeus' Song
[Tune: Tallis' Canon]

1. I praise my God that I can see
   All that the Lord has done for me.
   For I was blind and now I see
   All that the Lord has done for me.

2. In my deepest darkness I was lost,
   Until my savior's path I crossed.
   Then I was blind, but now I see
   All that the Lord has done for me.

3. I called the name of Jesus loud,
   He heard me over all the crowd.
   He touched my eyes and now I see
   All that the Lord has done for me.

4. And from this day my voice I raise,
   To give my savior thanks and praise;
   Though I were blind, I still could see
   All that the Lord has done for me. Amen.

FOURTH SUNDAY IN LENT

Sermon

"Just Ask!"

"Go your way; your faith has made you well."
Mark 10:52

Jesus healed people. He spent much of his time healing people, and sent his disciples out to heal. Jesus healed — we do not. For most of us in mainline Protestantism, healing is an embarrassment. We associate it with tent meetings and hucksterism, Elmer Gantry and Jimmy Swaggart. Yet, Jesus said: "Go, heal." Have we surrendered too much, not because we reject Jesus' command to us to heal, but because we reject the associations healing has taken on in the last 100 years, the quacks, the phonies, the shouting and frenzy? I wonder. Let's try to forget for a few minutes everything we know about faith-healing as it has been practiced in our century — the frauds, the embarrassments, the scandals. Let us try to think only about this healing, this story of Bartimaeus. Let us seek to discover how Jesus would have us heal and be healed.

What do we know about Bartimaeus? We don't even know his name, for bar-Timaeus simply means that he was the son of Timaeus. He was blind. He was a beggar. He lived and begged in the city of Jericho, an oasis that was the Palm Springs of Judea. But is there anything else we know about him? Well, we know that he was persistant. "Jesus, son of David, have mercy on me!" He was not happy to be a blind beggar. He was so unhappy that when he cried out and was put down by his betters who told him to be quiet, that didn't stop him for a moment. He cried again and again: "Son of David, have mercy on me!"

48

Mercy? What is mercy to a blind beggar? A few shekels? Taking him off the streets and giving him shelter? A welfare program? Mercy? What kind of mercy does he need? And what driving need led him to cry out that way? Now I'm going to ask you to make a big jump. For a moment, be Bartimaeus. I know it's hard; we have sight, we are not beggars. But it is possible to empathize and understand Bartimaeus at some level. We are all in some way in need. There are ways and times for all of us in which we are blind. We all, in our time, have cried out in some way for mercy. So be Bartimaeus and feel how great your need would have to be to lead you to cry out against all resistance: "Jesus, Son of David, have mercy on me!" That's not easy, is it? But can you begin to understand what it took for Bartimaeus to call out that day?

And Jesus stopped — and turned — and answered. "What do you want me to do for you?" When we call out to Jesus for mercy and forgiveness, he asks what we want him to do for us. Bartimaeus knew: "Master, let me receive my sight." Sounds easy to ask for? It's not. But why? Why is it hard for a blind man to ask for sight? Why is it hard for us to ask for what we really want and need the most? We have been taught to pray for what is proper, to circle all around the issue, to pray prayers that are so general and so passive. Jesus is aggressive in prayer: "Give us this day!" "Deliver us from evil!" "Let this cup pass." Why do we, who are sick, find it so hard to ask for healing? Could we be afraid that the answer might be no? Maybe it is better sometimes not to know — when to ask for the best means facing the worst: that no healing will come. Perhaps we do not heal as Jesus healed because we are afraid to fail. Afraid that God will fail to hear us no matter how loud we cry.

Jesus answered Bartimaeus: "Go your way; your faith has made you well." What has made him well? Wasn't it Jesus who made him well? Jesus said: "Your faith has made you well." What does that mean? Does it mean that all you have to do is to be a good Christian and believe the right things and everything will be okay? That God takes care of the upright? "Your

49

faith has made you well." What does that say about healing? Take a look at some whose faith made them well. One was a leper, "unclean," an outcast. Another was a centurion, a Roman, one of the oppressors, the occupying army, the secret police. There was a woman with a hemorrhage who touched Jesus and "defiled" him. And Jarius, a "ruler," one of the establishment, those who had the least time for Jesus. And finally Bartimaeus, crying "Son of David" just like the Palm Sunday crowd would a few days later. And he did not understand any more about Jesus than they did. What did all these whose faith made them well have in common? Certainly not belief or doctrine. Some were Jews and some pagans; some knew quite a lot about Jesus and some nothing at all. The only thing they had in common was that they asked. They did not just ask, they cried out. And when they were told to shut up, they cried out again. They asked the impossible. They knew Jesus had what they needed and they demanded it from him. For them, faith was not gentle and long-suffering, faith was persistent, aggressive, bold, brassy and demanding. And Jesus heard and turned around. "Your faith has made you well." Just ask.

It is a paradox, isn't it? Healing faith is the ability to ask for the one thing you want so much that you are scared to death to ask for it. Even to say it, even to think it, is to face the painful possibility that the answer might be no. Sometimes that is just too hard; to risk, to gamble everything. It is easier to give in, to be fatalistic, to go mourning to your grave. We do that all the time. We allow our needs — our blindness, our illnesses of body and mind and spirit, to control us. We feel conspired against, sold out, helpless, driven by fate, lost and alone. And it is hard to cry out, to spring up, to ask.

You can't make it alone. It helps to have a few people around, like the church. People who will laugh and cry with you. People who will hold your hand and care for you. People who will say: "Take heart, rise; he is calling you." But, even with that, then it is up to you. "What do you want me to do for you?" Do you ask; against all odds, do you ask the

50

impossible? Do you say, "I choose to live as a well, whole, healed person?" Knowing the answer might be no? Faith! And maybe that is where healing starts. You hit bottom and find God there, too. And maybe your eyes don't get healed, but your life is healed and becomes strong and healthy and full of vision. And maybe . . .

Jesus said, "Go your way, you are well," and it was so. But Bartimaeus did not go his way. Bartimaeus, healed and whole, followed him on the way, the way to the cross.

FIFTH SUNDAY IN LENT

Call To Worship
Prayer Of Confession
Hymn
Sermon

FIFTH SUNDAY IN LENT

Call To Worship
Adapted From Ezekiel 37:11-14

L: Then he said to me, ''Son of Man, these bones are the whole house of Israel. Behold, they say,

R: 'Our bones are dried up, and our hope is lost, we are clean cut off . . .'

L: Thus says the Lord God: Behold I will open your graves, O my people; and I will bring you home . . .

R: And I will put my spirit within you, and you shall live; then you shall know that I, the Lord, have spoken.

L: And I have done it, says the Lord.''

FIFTH SUNDAY IN LENT

Prayer Of Confession

Lord, we confess that in our world Lazarus has died, and we are without hope. We have tried to serve you and serve your people; yet anger and pride, prejudice and greed increase. We have grown weary in the struggle for justice and peace, and our future seems to us dry as dust. Come, Lord, and summon from within us deep wellsprings of thanks and praise. May your life-giving spirit wash over us like streams in the desert, granting us forgiveness and calling us to live with you. In the name of Jesus Christ, who raises us with Lazarus, from death to life. Amen.

Assurance Of Forgiveness (adapted from Ezekiel 37:14): "I have done it, says the Lord." Your sins are forgiven, live in Christ. Amen.

Scripture: John 11:1-7, 17, 20-27, 32-34

FIFTH SUNDAY IN LENT

Hymn
[Tune: Austrian Hymn, often sung as
"Glorious Things of Thee Are Spoken"]

1. Deeply bound in death's dark caverns,
   Lazarus slept in the grave.
   Jesus came when hope had faded,
   Late to heal, too late to save.
   Yet he called unto his Father,
   Gave thanks for what God had done.
   "Lazarus, come forth my brother!
   Death's strong bonds from you undone."

2. Dry and hopeless, Lord you found me,
   Martha, Mary were my kin.
   Emptiness and pain had bound me;
   Dead without and dead within.
   Then your word of life was spoken,
   Called me forth and told me "Live!"
   All my bondage then was broken,
   Death to death and life to give.

3. Jesus Christ, the resurrection,
   Life to all who call his name;
   Who believe, in his protection,
   Life and death are both the same.
   Glory, glory to the Father,
   Glory, glory to the Son,
   Glory to God's Holy Spirit,
   Ever three and ever one. Amen.

FIFTH SUNDAY IN LENT

Sermon

"Dry Bones And Live Hope"

"Father, I thank You that You have heard me."
John 11:41

Jesus had a friend. The name of his friend was Lazarus. When you have a friend, and your friend needs help, you do what you can. So when Lazarus was ill, naturally they sent to Jesus for help. "You have healed others, why not your friend?" But Jesus did not do what they thought he would do. "This illness is not unto death; it is for the glory of God," and he went about his business.

Yet Lazarus' illness was to the death. Jesus was late and when he finally arrived, Lazarus was dead, and Jesus wept. There are those who claim that Jesus purposely allowed Lazarus to die so that he might work a great miracle. I don't believe that at all, for Jesus wept. He broke down and cried because he had lost a friend, and it hurt. He mourned the death of his friend.

Mary didn't help him in his grief. Listen to what Mary said to Jesus: "Lord, if you had been here, my brother would not have died." Which is to say, "Lord, why weren't you here?" I want you to listen to Mary, because we have been there, every one of us! We have been there with Mary. There is nothing harder to understand than death, especially sudden death, especially the death of a friend. "Why?" "Why did he have to die?" "Why weren't you here?" Mary wants an answer — "Jesus, why didn't you do something?" Mary wants an answer, and there is no answer.

How is Mary's question our question? When we come face to face with the death of someone we love, some very primitive fears arise — and they are often fears for ourselves. These fears attack the very framework of our lives, the structure which helps us make sense out of life. The supporting structure of Mary's life had as its foundation an assumption which went something like this: "We are friends of Jesus, Jesus will protect us from harm." But Lazarus died, and the framework of Mary's life came tumbling down. She had lost her brother, but she had also lost the structure which enabled her to make sense out of life. As she faced the irreversible, physical evidence of Lazarus' death, something inside her died as well.

In this world, there are many ways to die. Relationships die, belief withers, confidence in our own ability to cope evaporates, hopes for peace, health and happiness fade away before the harsh realities of life. Look around you, the evidence is there before your eyes that Lazarus is dead in our world as well: problems which defy solution . . . emptiness and loneliness and violence. Our Lazarus is dead and Jesus weeps for us, every one of us.

Then Jesus did one of the strangest things he would ever do. Even as he was weeping for his lost friend, against all the evidence that Lazarus was gone forever, Jesus trusted in God's promise and proclaimed life. "Lazarus, come out!" And it was so. It made no sense in the natural order of things, but it made perfect sense in terms of who Jesus was. Jesus prayed to his Father. The tense of Jesus' prayer is important. He did not pray, "Father, hear me." Rather, "Father, you have heard me." "I thank you, you have heard me." This was not intercession for the lost life of a friend, but thanksgiving for what God had already done. That Lazarus actually walked out of the tomb was coincidental — because Jesus was declaring that God's glory is in the world, and none of the old rules are in force any more. He who has ears to hear, let him hear!

Jesus helped Mary see that it is not just a matter of my faith being able to take care of me in a crisis; rather, the glory of God has already pronounced the death of all kinds of deaths.

When we are dried up, cut off, all hope lost, God says (to paraphrase the prophet Ezekiel): "I will bring you home, I will put my spirit in you, you will live!" When will this be? Off in the future? Up in heaven? No! "I have done it, says the Lord (Ezekiel 37:14)."

In the midst of the darkest, emptiest of our days, Jesus says to us: Come out! Live! Like Mary, we cannot be content unless we know. When we say, "Jesus, if you had only been there . . ." Then it is that he calls us to trust, not that everything will turn out for the best by-and-by, but that there is a new, freeing, life-giving creation in Jesus Christ. When we are like Lazarus, Jesus calls us and tells us that we need not be bound and entombed by the many deaths which bind us, not even by the fear of bodily death. He unbinds and frees us and calls us, saying, "Live!" In any of our deaths, whenever life emerges out of the tomb, it is because the glory of God has been poured out on our lives, and we can never be the same again. When you have been unbound, like Lazarus, from death and the fear of death, then you know that the greatest thing you can do in this world is proclaim the glory of God who brings us life. Yes, weep over the forces of death, but proclaim the life-giving glory of God with all your being.

Jesus says to you: "Come out! Live!"

"I have done it, says the Lord."

PALM
SUNDAY

Call To Worship
Prayer Of Confession
Hymn
Sermon

PALM SUNDAY

Call To Worship
Adapted From Zechariah 9:9, 10

L: Rejoice greatly, O daughter of Zion!

R: Shout aloud, O daughter of Jerusalem!

L: Lo, your king comes to you; triumphant and victorious is he,

R: Humble and riding on a donkey, on a colt, the foal of a donkey.

L: I will cut off the chariot from Ephraim and the war horse from Jerusalem;

R: And the battle bow shall be cut off, and he shall command peace to the nations.

PALM SUNDAY

Prayer Of Confession

O Lord, forgive us when the cries of "Hosanna!"
fall too easily from our lips. We know that we have
within us the potential to cry "Crucify!" as well.
May we not be so deafened by the roar of the crowd,
nor so blinded by the waving palms that we forget
your way leads to the cross. Forgive us for easy faith
and shallow praise. Make us followers of the way,
even the way of the cross. Amen.

Scripture: Luke 19:28-42

PALM SUNDAY

Hymn
[Tune: St. Stephen, often sung as
"The King Shall Come When Morning Dawns"]

1. "Hosanna to the King of Kings,"
   "Hosanna" loud we cried,
   Not knowing that our King of Kings
   Would soon be crucified.

2. We threw down garments on the road,
   With branches from the trees;
   But he would soon be lifted up,
   To die between two thieves.

3. O could those voices raised in praise
   On that Palm Sunday morn,
   Have cried on Friday, "Crucify!,"
   All full of hate and scorn?

4. So though we praise Palm Sunday now,
   The greater triumph still,
   Came when Christ faced both cross and grave
   To do the father's will. Amen.

PALM SUNDAY

Sermon

"On The Way To The Cross"

"And when they drew near and saw the city
he wept over it."
Luke 19:41

Palm Sunday is a hard day for preachers. At a breakfast gathering for clergy last week the question was asked, "Have you ever heard a good Palm Sunday sermon?" The consensus was no, we had not. We decided that perhaps part of the reason for that is that Palm Sunday is the crowd's day . . . Palm Sunday is the disciples' day . . . Palm Sunday is not Jesus' day. On Palm Sunday Jesus tried to say something which no one heard. Jesus had something to say and he said it by riding into Jerusalem on a donkey. Not a big white horse, not lifted high on the shoulders of triumphant disciples, but on a little donkey — feet dragging in the dust, robe flapping, what a sight! But who heard the statement he was making? The crowd had its own agenda. The crowd, the same crowd which in five short days would cry "crucify!" instead of "hosanna!;" the crowd wanted to shout in a messiah, any messiah, even an unlikely messiah on a donkey. "Maybe this one will do something about taxes and get the Romans off our backs. We only half believe it, we've heard it so many times before but . . . what the heck, what do we have to lose?" So grab a branch, wave it around and shout: "Blessed is the King who comes in the name of the Lord!" That was the crowd.

And the disciples? Disciples who in five short days would desert him, run away and hide? The disciples also had an agenda: "We're number 1, we're number 1! Disciples of Jesus, we're number 1! After all that walking, after all those dusty Galilean roads, finally we've hit the big time! We're playing Jerusalem, and look at the fans — It's a sell-out crowd!'' So grab a branch, wave it around and shout: "Hosanna! Blessed is the King who comes in the name of the Lord!'' Those were the disciples.

But Jesus? What did Jesus say on Palm Sunday? Amid all the hullabaloo and hosannas, we often forget that Jesus spoke. ''And when he drew near and saw the city, he wept over it, saying: 'Would that even today you knew the things that make for peace' (Mark 19:41-41).'' What happens on Palm Sunday if we listen to Jesus for a change, instead of the crowds; Jesus, instead of the disciples? It is not an empty question. We are celebrating our Lord entering Jerusalem. Without pushing the image too far, I think it is fair to say we are also celebrating Jesus entering our lives as well. We are trying our best, with trumpets and palms, to do it triumphantly. In the midst of celebrating disciples, shouting crowds, Jesus wept. People lined the streets, crying out, ''Hosanna! Deliver us! Save us! Give us peace in our time!'' He said, ''If you only knew today what is needed for peace.''

I suppose the first century search for peace, tranquility, prosperity and security was much like our own. Some, back then, depended on a stable government with just laws. Rome offered peace and stability. When we listen to candidates for public office, stability, security and prosperity is what we like to hear. We are not so different from the crowds. Television evangelism is booming. Bookstores are flooded with religious self-help books. Attendance in the crystal cathedrals of the nation is growing. We are not so different from the disciples. If we compare the first century search with our own, the similarities are almost frightening: they had mystery cults as fervent as the Moonies, eastern cults as esoteric as the Hari Krishna, sacred knowledge groups that would put our faith-healers to shame, and zealots as right-wing as neo-Nazis, as nationalistic as PLO terrorists. And they all had an answer: ''Do you want peace? Then be a good citizen, read your Bible, send a contribution, go to church. Follow Rev. Moon, meditate with the Bagwan, have your consciousness raised, blow your enemies to hell." Jesus wept.

What did he see that his disciples did not? He knew his fate was sealed when he entered the gates of Jerusalem, adoring crowds or no crowds. Jesus wept. He knew the finely tuned justice of Rome would go amazingly blind at the critical moment. He knew the biblical fundamentalists would seek to kill him. He knew the religious liberals would seek to kill him. He knew the laws of his country would not protect him. Jesus wept.

Jesus wept . . . and still he spoke of peace. What did he see that we don't? What does he want us to hear that we can't seem to comprehend? We know by now that his peace has nothing to do with national security. We know that his peace has nothing to do with how strong our faith is or how happy we are. The day he spoke of peace was the beginning of a week which ended with a last supper, a public humiliation, death on a cross. How morbid . . . for Palm Sunday. Yet Jesus Christ, on this day, spoke of peace. The disciples, on this day, wanted to hear anything else except the kind of peace he meant, for his peace would come from doing the will of God which was the cross. The disciples could not hear it. Security was not a cross. Tranquility was not a cross. Prosperity was not a cross . . . not a cross of Jesus! Though Jesus told them over and over that he must go to Jerusalem, that he must suffer, that he must die . . . they never heard. All the securities they clung to as they celebrated in triumph that Palm Sunday kept them from hearing Jesus.

I don't know if we are any further along than the disciples in our ability to hear Jesus this day. What do we need from Jesus which blocks us from hearing him this Palm Sunday? "Would that even today you knew the things that make for peace!" His peace comes from the very things we want to flee. His peace comes to those who take on the suffering, who take on the hurt, who take on the alienation of the world. Peace? That's not my peace, that's not my kind of peace! Jesus wept.

What do you need from Jesus? Security . . . let it go. Happiness . . . let it go. Health, well-being . . . let it go. Success . . . let it go. Starting now, through the supper on Thursday, the horror of Friday, the despair of Saturday, try to follow along with your Lord and hear what Jesus has to say to you. Perhaps then, even in the midst of a Palm Sunday celebration, we will begin, just begin, to know what is needed for peace. His peace.

MAUNDY THURSDAY

The Passover Meal Of The Last Supper

A Communion Service

MAUNDY THURSDAY

The Passover Meal Of The Last Supper
A Communion Service

This communion may be celebrated around tables or in the pews. It is possible for a meal to be served as part of the celebration, but not necessary to the service. This is not, strictly speaking, a Seder in the traditional sense, for many of the Seder traditions are rooted in the diaspora of post-biblical times. Rather, this is a celebration of the Lord's Supper which includes some traditional Hebrew Passover prayers and symbolic actions to help Christians understand the context of Jesus' last supper with his disciples, as it is described in the Gospel of Mark.

Prologue (from Mark 14:12-16)

L: And on the first day of unleavened bread, when they sacrificed the Passover lamb, his disciples said to him:

R: **Where will you have us go and prepare for you to eat the Passover?**

L: And he sent two of his disciples and said to them:

R: **Go into the city, and a man carrying a jar of water will meet you; follow him, and wherever he enters, say to the householder, "The teacher says, where is my guest room where I am to eat the Passover with my disciples?"**

L: And he will show you a large upper room, furnished and ready; there prepare for us.

R: **And the disciples set out and went to the city and found it as he had told them; and they prepared the Passover.**

The Lighting Of The Candles

(As a woman from the congregation lights two candles on the communion table or, if seated at tables, candles are lit on each table, the congregation prays in unison:)

O Lord of all creation, may your light shine upon us with the blessings of peace for all the peoples on this night of nights. Amen.

Hymn (tune: Communion Spiritual)

1. Let us break bread together, on this night, on this night;
   Let us break bread together, on this night, on this night.
   On this Passover night, as we eat the unleavened bread,
   O Lord, draw near unto us.

2. Let us drink wine together, on this night, on this night;
   Let us drink wine together, on this night, on this night.
   On this Passover night, as we eat the unleavened bread,
   O Lord, draw near unto us.

3. Let us praise God together, on this night, on this night;
   Let us praise God together, on this night, on this night.
   On this Passover night, as we sing to the Lord our God,
   O Lord draw near unto us. Amen.

Scripture: Mark 14:17-21

Meditation

"On the night before his death, our Lord Jesus took bread . . ." We've known those words all our lives. The very familiarity of the Lord's supper can sometimes be a block to our understanding. For one thing, we may not understand that it was not a unique nor an unusual thing for Jesus to take bread and break it and give it to them to eat. Every sabbath, every holiday was celebrated with the breaking of bread. The accounts of the last supper may seem sketchy to us: "Said a prayer . . . sang a hymn . . ." This is because the gospel writer did not need to record these traditional prayers and hymns which were as familiar to his readers as the breaking and sharing of bread. Just as we know that a service of worship will almost always include hymns, Scripture and prayer and of course, an offering, so those early Christians knew from experience that a festival supper for the holy days would include blessings everyone knew by heart, washing hands, breaking bread, sharing cups of wine.

Breaking of bread and sharing of cup was nothing new with Jesus. When Jesus gave them bread and a cup he was doing just what they expected him to do; and just what he knew they would keep on doing, week after week, when he was gone — every holiday meal, every sabbath meal. Jesus took an action which his disciples had known since childhood and, at the passover meal, the feast of freedom, he transformed it by saying: "This is my body . . . this is my blood of the covenant which is poured out for many (Mark 14:22, 24)." They would keep on breaking bread and drinking a cup together anyway; now they would perform this familiar action remembering him.

The world was about to dis-member him. The events of that night and the dark hours of Friday would dis-member his disciples as well. For, as he said, when his enemies "strike the shepherd, the sheep will be scattered (Mark 14:27)." The horror of the cross sent his disciples scurrying to crawl into the deepest hole they could find. Perhaps Jesus knew that they would need something like this familiar, comforting, everyday action to come to an understanding of his sacrifice on the cross. The memory of the very breaking of his body and spilling of his blood which dis-membered them would pull them back together as they remembered him. No longer captives of their own fears, they would be set free even as God's ancient people had been freed from slavery. In eating the solid goodness of the bread, in drinking the wine of the cup, they would remember him and know he was with them forever.

As we gather here tonight to share this meal in our holy days of cross and resurrection, we are also brought back together as we remember him. Wherever our lives have wandered, however far from his pathways we have strayed, Christ waits at this table to call us home and free us for his service.

Washing Of Hands

L: Let us gather at his table and wash away the burdens and the sins which we bring with us to the house of the Lord. Let us wash our hands, as we know our lives are washed clean by the blood of the Lamb. *Baruch ata adonai elohainu melech ha-olam asher kidshanu b-mitzvotov v'tzivanu al netilat yadayim.*

R: **Blessed are you, Lord God, sovereign of the universe. You have blessed us with your commandments and instructed us in the washing of our hands.**

(Bowl and towel are passed for all to wash hands.)

L: At the last supper, we are told that Jesus took the bowl and the cloth and went himself to wash, not their hands, but their feet; fixing in their minds and in ours for all time that the followers of Jesus Christ, like their master, are the servants of the servants of God.

The Haggadah

(The youngest person in the room asks:) Why is this night different from every other night?

The people respond in unison from Deuteronomy 26:5-9):
Wandering Arameans were our fathers and mothers; and they went down into Egypt and sojourned there, few in number; and there they became a nation: great, mighty and populous. And the Egyptians treated us harshly, and laid upon us harsh bondage. Then we cried to the Lord, the God of our Ancestors, and the Lord heard our voice, and saw our affliction, our toil and our oppression; and the Lord brought us out of Egypt with a mighty hand and an outstretched arm, with great terror, with signs and wonders. And God brought us into this place and to this land, a land flowing with milk and honey.

Hymn (tune: Eventide, most often sung as "Abide With Me")

1. When we were slaves, God called us to be free,
   Hope for the hopeless, led us through the sea.
   Strengthened, renewed, in God's commandments strong,
   Wilderness people sing a homeward song.

2. Now at our table on this night of nights,
   We drink the cup and light Passover lights.
   Bread of affliction, toil and misery,
   Broken to save us and to set us free.

3. Here with you, Lord, we eat this final meal,
   Your body broken, all our sins to heal,
   Your blood poured out for us upon the tree,
   The Lamb of God who died to make us free. Amen.

The Breaking Of Bread

L: This is the unleavened bread, the bread of affliction that reminds us of the slavery of our fathers and mothers in the land of Egypt. As we eat this bread together we remember that the Lord heard our cry and brought us out of slavery to freedom.

This is the unleavened bread of the Passover which Jesus gave to his disciples saying:
Baruch ata adonai elohainu melech ha-olam, ha-motzi lechem min ha-aretz.

R: **Blessed are you, Lord God, sovereign of the universe. You bring us bread from the earth.**

L: And as they were eating, he took bread and blessed and broke it and gave it to them, and said: "Take; this is my body (Mark 14:22)."

(Break, pass and eat the unleavened bread.)

Blessing And Sharing The Cup

L: And he took a cup, and when he had given thanks he gave it to them, and they drank all of it. Let us give thanks to the Lord our God.

R: **Praise the Lord!**

L: O give thanks to the Lord, for God is good.

R: **The steadfast love of the Lord endures forever.**

L: Let the redeemed of the Lord say so, whom God has redeemed from trouble and gathered in from the lands, from the east and from the west, from the north and from the south.

R: **Some wandered in desert wastes, hungry and thirsty, their soul fainted within them.**

L: Then they cried to the Lord in their trouble,

R: And God delivered them from their distress;

L: The Lord led them by a straight way, till they reached a city to dwell in.

R: Let them give thanks for God's steadfast love, for God satisfies the thirsty and fills the hungry with good things.

L: Blessed be the Lord, the God of Israel, from everlasting to everlasting!

R: And let all the people say "Amen!" Praise the Lord!

(From Psalms 106, 107)

L: *Baruch ata adonai elohainu melech ha-olam borai pri hagofen.*

R: Blessed are you, Lord God, sovereign of the universe. You create the fruit of the vine.

L: And he said to them, "This is my blood of the covenant which is poured out for many. Truly I say to you, I shall not drink again of the fruit of the vine until that day when I drink it new in the Kingdom of God (Mark 14: 24, 25)."

(Share communion of the cup.)

Hymn: (tune Bunessan, often sung as "Morning Has Broken")

1. As they were eating, took bread and blessed it,
   Broke it apart and gave it to them.
   "This is my body, broken to save you."
   We eat this bread, remembering him.

2. He took a cup and gave thanks to heaven,
   "This is my blood, poured out for you all."
   In crucifixion, covenant given,
   We drink together, answer his call.

3. Now at your table, Lord dwell among us,
   Be with your people, share in the feast.
   Heal us, forgive us, free us and save us.
   Bring us together, grant us your peace.

4. This is the night of feasting and sorrow,
   Night of betrayal, night of despair.
   Table to garden, waiting the morrow,
   Lone and forsaken, cross waiting there. Amen.

Benediction

L: "And when they had sung a hymn, they went out to the Mount of Olives (Mark 14:26)."

On that first Maundy Thursday, the disciples went from the table to the cross. It is the cross which has brought us to this table tonight.

Our Passover meal has ended, and we are called again to follow our Lord.

> Follow in service.
> Follow in commitment.
> Follow in love for God, who first loved you.
> Follow Jesus the Christ.
> Follow your savior to the cross.

> Follow, and may the blessing of God:
> Father, Son and Holy Spirit
> go with you now and always. Amen.

GOOD FRIDAY TENEBRAE

A Service Of
Light And Shadow

GOOD FRIDAY
TENEBRAE

A Service Of Light And Shadow

About the service: Tenebrae, meaning "shadows," is a traditional service of candlelight and darkness for Good Friday. Twelve candles will be needed to represent the 12 disciples, and one large white candle to represent Christ. These may be in candelabra, but the use on the communion table of candles of assorted sizes and shapes and colors is particularly effective. Before the service, recruit 12 members of the congregation to put the disciples' candles out at the times indicated. The church should be in semi-darkness throughout, darkened further each time candles are extinguished, and completely dark as the Christ candle is removed. After a short period of darkness, some lights are restored for the congregation to leave. There should be a note in the bulletin asking the congregation to leave the sanctuary in complete silence.

Call To Worship (John 14:18-19)

L: Jesus said: "I will not leave you desolate: I will come to you.

R: Yet a little while, and the world will see me no more, but you will see me.

L: Because I live, you will live also.

Time Of Confession:

Spoken in Unison: **You have called us to follow you, Lord Jesus, but we are afraid. With your disciples we swear our** faithfulness, yet in the darkness of our hearts, we know our words are empty. We confess that we have within us the potential to betray you like Judas, deny you like Peter, desert you like all your disciples. Forgive us, Lord, for we are as they were. Fill us anew with the fiery confidence of your spirit, and renew in us the strength of your presence, that we, weak as we are, might be transformed into those who follow in spite of their fears. Help us to follow even to the cross. Amen.

Silent

Sung *(Note: If there is a choir for the service, an anthem with a penitential text is appropriate at this point. A suggestion would be "All We Like Sheep" from Handel's* **Messiah.**)

Assurance Of Forgiveness (From Ezekiel 34)

L: For thus says the Lord God: "Behold I, I myself will reach for my sheep, and will seek them out."

R: **"I will seek the lost, I will bring back the strayed, I will bind up the crippled, I will strengthen the weak, and the strong I will watch over."**

L: "And I, the Lord, will be their God." Amen.

Hymn (Suggestion: "Go To Dark Gethsemane")

The Traitor
Matthew 26:14-16, 20-25
The Judas candle is extinguished

Anthem Or Solo

The Betrayal In The Garden
Mark 14:32-50
The 10 disciples' candles are extinguished

Hymn (tune: Passion Chorale, often sung as "O Sacred Head")

1. Disciples who were faithful in Galilee's bright sun,
   All pledged to follow Jesus, their voices joined as one.
   All broke the bread together, all shared the cup with him,
   But in the garden's shadows, their faithfulness grew dim.

2. The darkness of the evening, descends upon us now.
   In morning's golden sunlight, we made our solemn vow,
   To follow Christ our savior, through trial, cross and grave.
   Our words ring in the darkness, more hollow now than
   brave.

3. With Judas we betray him, we sell ourselves for gain.
   And Peter's quick denial reflects our fear of pain.
   Our words, like theirs, were faithful, pledged heart and soul
   to him,
   Like them, in fear and trembling, our faith grows faint and
   dim.

4. O Jesus in the darkness, alone upon the cross,
   How often we betray you, how often feel the loss.
   Our dreams and hopes are scattered, like dust upon the wind,
   As throned in deepest darkness, your triumphs now begin.

5. God's presence never fails us, in darkness or in light,
   In splendor of the morning, or deep descending night;
   When we are true and faithful, or frightened, lone and lost,
   God with us in our sorrows, was with Christ on the cross.
   Amen.

Peter's Denial
Luke 22-54-62
Peter's candle is extinguished

Responsive Reading (From Psalm 139)

L: O Lord, you have searched me and known me!

R: You know when I sit down and when I rise up; you discern my thoughts from afar.

L: You are acquainted with all my ways.

R: Where could I go from your Spirit? Where could I flee from your presence?

L: If I ascend to heaven, you are there! If I make my bed in Sheol, you are there!

R: If I take the wings of the morning and dwell in the uttermost parts of the sea, even there your hand shall lead me, and your right hand will hold me.

L: If I say, "Let only darkness cover me, and the light about me be night."

R: Even the darkness is not dark to you, the night is light as the day; for darkness is as light with you.

L: How precious to me are your thoughts, O God! How vast is the sum of them!

R: If I could count them, they are more than the sand. And when I awake, I am still with you.

Hymn (Suggestion: "When I Survey the Wondrous Cross")

Meditation: "Darkness"

*". . . if I made my bed in Sheol, you are there
. . . even darkness is not dark to you."*
Psalm 139

Tonight, we move with Jesus from light to darkness. This is not an easy move for us, for we are creatures of the light, who rejoice in a God of light, in whom we see no darkness at all. We in fact seek to confine God to the light spaces of life, and thereby exclude God from our darkness. Happiness, love, healing, justice — this is what God is all about to us. Don't talk to us about pain, suffering, discipline, judgment — what has God to do with those?

Let me give you an easy demonstration of what I mean. Look around you. Do you see those empty pews on this Good Friday evening? They were full last Sunday, they will be full next Sunday. Where are all the people who are not here tonight to walk into this darkness with you and with Jesus? Think about last Sunday, Palm Sunday. A day of light. Certainly Palm Sunday has overtones of darkness, for we know that those who shouted "Hosanna!" will within the week be screaming "Crucify!" But we try our best to cover up that threatening dark with children's choirs and waving palms. How many of those who celebrated in the light last Sunday are missing tonight? Most of our congregation will avoid encountering darkness in this week of the cross; will, instead, go from light to light. They will go from the light of Palm Sunday directly to the light of Easter, never encountering the darkness of the cross along the way.

Is there no place in our faith for the experience of darkness? I am driven by the shadows of Holy Week to assert that God is in the darkness as well as the light. That is hard to hear, hard to comprehend, hard to absorb . . . God in darkness. I visited a woman in the hospital. All the signs pointed to a tumor growing in her body. As she waited for the results of the tests, she spoke words of faith and hope, of trust in God. A few days later, the results were in, the news was bad. She said: "I don't believe it, all my prayers were for nothing. I never thought God could let this happen to me." All her prayers had been focused on the expectation of healing, of cure, of light from God. When bad news plunged her into darkness, she was sure God had abandoned her. There was no room for God in her darkness.

In the story of Good Friday we read: ". . . there was darkness over the whole land." When my father was dying, I visited him often in his hospital room. I know that I was there all hours of the day, yet in my memory, that room is always dark; the eternal twilight of a place in which people move softly and speak with hushed voices; harsh overhead light turned off, soft glow of light behind the bed, and the feeble sparkling colors of a ceramic Christmas tree on his bedside table. The darkness of that room, in my memory, is the darkness of his dying. Cancer had stolen his voice, his strength, and now his life. I was a professional, comforter at a thousand bedsides, but I had no words for my father. In his darkness, heavy darkness, I was numb. ". . . there was darkness over the whole land."

Even as I was lost in my father's darkness, I cannot comprehend the darkness which enfolded Jesus on the cross. I cannot speak of this darkness without somehow trying to lighten it. I make apologies, excuses for God, God who could consign his son to darkness. On Easter we will likely sing that Jesus "endured the cross and grave, sinner to redeem and save." We will sing as though the cross was nothing more than a temporary inconvenience; something like a trip to the dentist, painful but endurable if over quickly and the end result makes the pain worthwhile. At worst, I reason, God was absent from the cross that dark Friday. Perhaps, I rationalize, God handed Jesus over to the principalities and powers for a time, a sacrifice to save the world. But the thought of God dwelling in darkness, even the darkness which enfolded Jesus on the cross; the thought of such darkness leaves me stunned, speechless! But

. . . what if God was not absent? What if God was there, even there in the cross, in the pain, in the darkness?

When my father was dying, as he entered the coma which was his final darkness, he became angry. He was weak, his voice in the darkness less than a whisper. I don't remember the words, for it was the worst moment of my life. I do remember the feeling: I could leave that hospital room and go on with my life. He felt abandoned, deserted, alone in the darkness.

Jesus was alone, betrayed by Judas, denied by Peter, deserted by the rest. Jesus was abandoned . . . but was Jesus alone? God could not stand between Jesus and the darkness, holding off the pain, protecting him from death. So where was God on that terrible Friday? God was in the darkness with Jesus.

The message of Good Friday, for those of us who do not rush to leap from light to light, is that God is even in the darkness. Jesus' death focused the darkness around the cross unto an explosion of God's presence in the world. The curtain of the temple was torn apart. The deep darkness of God's house was dispersed, unleashed over the earth. The God of peace and light penetrated this world through violence and death and deep darkness.

God is in the darkness. God is in the darkness of a hospital room. God is in the darkness of bad news. God is in the darkness of his people's pain. God was even in the silent darkness of my father's dying. God is, in fact, in my light and in my darkness. God is in your joy and in your sorrow. God is, without apology in both our laughter and our tears. God does not stand between us and pain, holding it off, bringing only good news, but God is with us in the darkness. God is with us in our darkness when we feel most alone; especially when we are most alone. God is even in our darkness. ". . . if I make my bed in Sheol, you are there . . . even darkness is not dark to you."

Hymn *(Note: Since this hymn needs to be sung in almost total darkness, choose one most of the congregation will know, and have a choir or strong soloist for the congregation to follow. A suggestion which works well is "Were You there When They Crucified My Lord?" — with the words to each verse announced before they are sung.)*

The Crucifixion
Mark 15:22-39
The Christ candle is removed to return on Easter morning

We ask you to leave the sanctuary
in silence
as you think on the death
of Christ our Lord
and wait the resurrection.
Amen.

EASTER SUNDAY

Call To Worship
Prayer Of Confession
Hymn
Sermon

EASTER SUNDAY

Call To Worship
Adapted In Part From
1 Corinthians 15 and Colossians 3

L: Christ is risen!

R: The Lord is risen indeed!

L: Christ has been raised from the dead, the first fruits of those who have fallen asleep.

R: For as in Adam all die, so also in Christ shall all be made alive.

L: If then you have been raised with Christ, seek the things that are above.

R: When Christ who is our life appears, then we also will appear with him in glory.

EASTER SUNDAY

Prayer Of Confession

We praise you, O God, for those who have not seen, yet have believed. We thank you for Good Friday people who were not afraid to follow your Son from cross to grave. For the centurion who crucified him, yet believed; for Joseph of Arimathea, who condemned him, yet claimed his body for burial; for the women who stood by his cross when all the men had fled. Forgive us, when we need the glory of Easter morning to bring us to faith; when we need to see in order to believe. Grant us the faith of those who believed even before the resurrection. Amen.

Scripture: Mark 15:37-47 and 16:1-6

EASTER SUNDAY

Hymn
[Tune: Sine Nomine, often sung as
"For All The Saints"]

1. Sing to the Lord, on resurrection day;
   From cross to tomb, we follow on Christ's way,
   Your faithful people, here to praise and pray.
   For Easter wonder! Alleluia!

2. For three sad days our lives were full of fears.
   Behind closed doors, our hopes were lost in tears.
   Now with the dawning, Christ our Lord appears.
   For Easter wonder! Alleluia!

3. Through all our days, God's love for us is strong,
   Our past and future to the Lord belong.
   Unto our God we raise this resurrection song.
   For Easter wonder! Alleluia!

4. Sing to the Lord, resounding hymns of praise;
   May all our days be resurrection days!
   Now let us join, and all our voices raise.
   For Easter wonder! Alleluia! Amen.

EASTER SUNDAY

Sermon

"Good Friday People In An Easter World"

"the centurion . . .
women . . . who followed him,
. . . Joseph of Arimathea, a respected member
of the council"
from Mark 15

He was a good friend of mine. "I've got a problem," he said. "I don't know what to believe. I don't even know if I believe. You see," he said, "I'm a pretty average sort of person. I've lived a pretty normal sort of life. Nothing much bad has ever happened to me, but nothing all that miraculous has ever happened to me either. So I don't know what to believe; I don't know what to believe about God. If I could experience some kind of miracle, then I could probably believe."

In the gospels, there are two kinds of people who believe. There are Easter people, those who experienced the wonder and mystery of the empty tomb, and believed: "My Lord and my God!" Most of us, including my friend, would like to be Easter people. The excitement, the spiritual uplift, the vibrant certainty of an Easter morning seems to be what we need to bring us to faith or to solidify our faith. But, like my friend, most of us have never been given the opportunity to experience Easter first hand. Most of us have lived pretty normal lives; pretty normal lives spiritually as well, with little first hand experience of the miraculous. Most of us must believe in a different way; believe without proof, believe with a faith that does not wait for Easter. In this we are in good company, for in the Gospel of Mark this morning we meet some people who did not need to experience Easter morning in order to be faithful. Mark introduces us to some Good Friday people who lived with Jesus through the pain, not the triumph; and, for them, that was enough, enough for faith.

Who are these Good Friday people in an Easter world? Think back for a minute. Remember the events of that Friday we now call good. Who stood by Jesus through the darkness of the cross? His disciples? Most likely his disciples, Peter and John and the rest? Yes? . . . NO! Mark's gospel is very definite in telling the tale when Mark says:

all the disciples drank the cup in the upper room,
all the disciples promised to die for Jesus,
all the disciples forsook him and fled.

They ran away. They all ran for their lives and left Jesus alone. Did none of those who followed Jesus on the long road from Galilee also follow him to the cross? Well, yes, there were followers of Jesus faithful enough to stand by the cross. Mark mentions them in chapter 15:

There were also women looking on . . . among whom as Mary Magdalene, and Mary the mother of James, and Salome . . . who, when he was in Galilee, followed him and many other women who came up with him to Jerusalem (Mark 15:40, 41).

Only the women, who were not even thought worthy in their time to be called disciples, stood by Jesus at the cross. The men were full of brave words, but when the time of testing came, they were not there. While the women watched, the men were hiding away, waiting. They were waiting for Easter and for faith. The women of Good Friday were already faithful.

But there were others who were full of faith that day. The most unlikely others you could possibly imagine. The only person at the cross to speak of faith was a Roman soldier who proclaimed: "Truly, this was the Son of God!" Why was a Roman soldier at the cross? The only reason a Roman soldier was at the cross was to crucify! The only words of faith at the cross were spoken by the soldier who crucified Jesus! Can you think of a more unlikely person to speak words of Good Friday faith? Yet he did!

And finally, another faithful person came to the cross that day. He came when Jesus was dead. He came to claim Jesus' body for burial in his own tomb. His name was Joseph of Arimathea, and he is honored in our memories for his Good Friday faith. Yet, who was Joseph? Mark states that he was an honored member of the council. And in the previous chapter, Mark says twice, just to be sure that we have heard, that the whole council condemned Jesus to death. The whole council condemned Jesus? Including that honored member of the council, Joseph of Arimathea?

These are the Good Friday people. These are Mark's faithful witnesses at the cross: a Jew who condemned Jesus, a Roman who pounded in the nails, women who were not afraid to watch him die. These unlikely people did not need the resurrection to call them to faith, for they were filled with the power of the cross. These Good Friday people were transformed by that power, a power great enough to turn even the most unlikely people into followers of the way.

I think Mark worried about the disciples of Jesus who ran and fled and hid away on Good Friday; disciples who needed the experience of Easter morning to call them back to faith. I think God worries about all Easter people, like those who were intrigued and attracted by Jesus' miracles, ran from the pain and despair of the cross, and then were drawn back to faith by the miracle of the resurrection. I think God worries about us, when we look to Jesus for a way out of our troubles, as a path to self-fulfillment or a guide to successful living; when the presence of God in our "normal" life just doesn't seem to be enough and we go off looking for some spiritual excitement or enlightenment, some spiritual high which will "help us believe."

Mark's gospel contains very few words about the resurrection, but chapters about the cross. To be sure, Mark believes in the resurrection of Jesus. Mark believes in the resurrection completely, but knows that the cross, not the tomb, is at the center of faith. The resurrection did not "complete" the cross, to give the story a happy ending. The resurrection simply confirmed the words of the Roman soldier: "This man was the Son of God." The resurrection is like the light bulb flashing on in the brain, the "ah-ha!", the "yes, of course!" to let others see what Good Friday people already knew. The resurrection is the bridge from the cross to a future of cross-bearing. That future is open to all, not just to the insiders, the experts in faith, those who have experienced a miracle. For the insiders, the disciples and friends, they all ran away before the cross. They left Good Friday people, people just like us: normal people, plain ordinary peoople. They left unlikely followers, the Roman, Joseph, the women — people who, without the miracle of Easter, discovered for themselves an extraordinary faith.

So what do I say to my friend? That we are, all of us, Good Friday people in an Easter world. That in a skeptical world which wants to see proof, which says, "give me a miracle and I'll believe," we are called to have faith in the Lord of the cross. For that Lord comes to us when we hurt, stands by us when we weep, lifts us up in our pain and comforts us in our loss. Oh, and who is also, by the way, the Lord of Easter, of empty tomb and alleluias!